with
PERMISSION

A Child's Guide to Understanding Consent

Hello!
My name is
Baya.

Hello!
My name is
Bash.

Book illustrations by Edyta Karaban

ISBN 978-1-957643-06-9 Paperback
ISBN 978-1-957643-04-5 Hardcover
ISBN 978-1-957643-05-2 eBook

Library of Congress Control Number: 2022908664

Published by Danidow Publishing LLC

Danidow Publishing LLC
Myrtle Beach, SC
USA
www.danidowpublishing.com

Dedication

To my mother Paulette
my best friend in this life
and next
I love you forever

With my permission, you may hug me;
touch my face or my hair.

With my permission, you may have a bite of my sandwich; sometimes I like to share.

With my permission, you may borrow my toys otherwise do not touch.

With my permission, you can help me learn Polish, Jamaican or Dutch.

With my permission, you can be a shoulder for me to lean on when I am down.

With my permission, you can be a friend and you may hang around.

With my permission, yes is now no
and that, my dear, is just fine.

With my permission, I will tell you all about my day.

With my permission, sometimes I do not feel like talking and that is quite okay.

With your permission,
this book has come to an end.

About the Author

Danielle Dowie is a teacher, writer, track and field analyst, and the author of Waa Gwaan Jimi: Welcome to the Jungle. She is the creator of Danidow Publishing LLC, an ambitious independent publishing platform specializing in storybooks for children. To learn more about Danielle and her work, go to:

www.danidowpublishing.com